Ireland and the
Land Question 1800–1922

Ireland and the
Land Question 1800–1922

Michael J. Winstanley

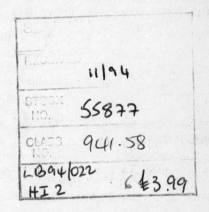

METHUEN · LONDON AND NEW YORK

First published in 1984 by
Methuen & Co. Ltd
11 New Fetter Lane,
London EC4P 4EE

Published in the USA by
Methuen & Co.
in association with Methuen, Inc.
733 Third Avenue, New York,
NY 10017

© 1984 Michael J. Winstanley

Typeset in Great Britain by
Scarborough Typesetting Services
and printed by
Richard Clay (The Chaucer Press)
Bungay, Suffolk

British Library Cataloguing in
Publication Data

Winstanley, Michael
Ireland and the land question
1800–1922 – (Lancaster pamphlets)
1. Land tenure – Ireland – History
2. Land tenure – Political aspects
– Ireland
I. Title   II. Series
333.3' 23' 09415   HD625
ISBN 0–416–37420–4

Contents

Foreword

Lancaster Pamphlets offer concise and up-to-date accounts of major historical topics, primarily for the help of students preparing for Advanced Level examinations, though they should also be of value to those pursuing introductory courses in universities and other institutions of higher education. They do not rely on prior textbook knowledge. Without being all-embracing, their aims are to bring some of the central themes or problems confronting students and teachers into sharper focus than the textbook writer can hope to do; to provide the reader with some of the results of recent research which the textbook may not embody; and to stimulate thought about the whole interpretation of the topic under discussion.

At the end of this pamphlet is a numbered list of the recent or fairly recent works that the writer considers most relevant to his subject. Where a statement or a paragraph is particularly indebted to one or more of these works, the number is given in the text. This serves at the same time to acknowledge the writer's source and to show the reader where he may find a more detailed exposition of the point concerned.

Guide to
major political events
and economic trends

1760s	beginning of expansion of corn growing
1778	Catholics allowed to own land
1780	population 4 million (estimate)
1782	Grattan's Parliament established in Dublin
1780s/1790s	conflict between Protestant Peep O'Day Boys and Catholic Defenders
1793–1815	French wars
	rapid expansion of Irish corn exports to England
1798	United Irishmen's abortive rebellion
1800	Act of Union abolishes Dublin parliament, allows Irish MPs to sit at Westminster and ends trade barriers.
1815	end of French wars leads to collapse of corn prices, beginning of expansion of pastoral farming and of substantial Irish emigration
1810s/1820s	collapse of domestic textile industry
	increasing poverty and reliance on potato for subsistence
1816	Ejectment Act makes process for legal eviction easier
1821	population c.6.7 million
1820s/1845	widespread rural unrest (Whiteboyism)
1823	O'Connell's Catholic Association formed to fight for right of Catholics to sit as MPs and hold public office (emancipation)

1826	Subletting Act attempts to stamp out subletting
1829	Catholic Emancipation Act
1836	Irish Constabulary formed
1838	Poor Law introduced into Ireland
1841	population *c*.8.2 million
	O'Connell's National Repeal Association established
1844	Young Ireland movement breaks away from O'Connell
	Devonshire Commission report
1845–9	1845 partial failure of potato crop
	1846–9 complete failure of crop leads to widespread deaths, evictions and emigration
1848	Young Ireland's abortive rebellion
1849	Encumbered Estates Act leads to massive land sales
	Tenant League formed demanding three 'Fs'
1851	population 6.4 million
1852–8	parliamentary party based on Tenant League
c.1851–76	increasing agricultural prosperity based on favourable price trends, low rents and specialized pastoral farms
1858	Irish Republican Brotherhood (Fenianism) formed in USA and Dublin
1860	Cardwell Act stipulates that only written agreements, not customary rights, would be recognized in courts of law
	Deasy Act allows for some compensation for tenants' improvements
1867	unsuccessful Fenian revolt
1868	Liberals win general election
	Gladstone's 'mission' to pacify Ireland
1869	Irish Church (Protestant) disestablished
1870	Land Act gives legal recognition to tenants' rights, provides for compensation and includes minor provisions relating to tenant purchase of farms
	Home Rule Confederation formed by Isaac Butt
1872	Secret Ballot
1874	Conservatives win general election; 59 Home Rule candidates returned
1877	Gladstone visits Ireland
1877–9	potato crops fail in the west
1879	beginning of Land War in the west

1879	June: 'New Departure'
	October: formation of Irish Land League
1879–80	agricultural depression deepens and spreads
1880	January–March: Parnell and Dillon tour the USA
	April: Liberals win general election
	September: boycotting adopted as league tactic
	Bessborough Commission appointed
1881	January: Bessborough Commission report
	March: Protection of Person and Property Act
	August: Land Act grants three 'Fs'
	October: Parnell and other leaders arrested
	'No Rent Manifesto'
	suppression of Land League
1882	May: Kilmainham Treaty – release of Parnell
	August: Arrears Act extends 1881 provisions to tenants in arrears with their rent
	collapse of land agitation
	October: Irish National League founded
1885	general election sees return of 85 Parnellite Irish MPs, plus one for a Liverpool constituency
	Gladstone declares in favour of Home Rule
	Conservatives pass Ashbourne Act providing £5 million for loans to tenants wishing to purchase their farms
1886	defeat of first Home Rule bill; split in Liberal Party
1887–91	Arthur Balfour Irish Secretary
1888	Land Purchase Act provides additional £5 million
late 1880s–1900s	revival of agricultural fortunes
1891	Land Act provides £33 million for tenant purchase and establishes Congested Districts Board
1896	amendments to act of 1891
1901	population c.4.5 million
1903	Wyndham Act greatly improves conditions for land purchase and leads to massive transfer of land
1909	Birrell Act increases funds for purchase
1916	Easter uprising
1920	Government of Ireland Act partitions the country
1921	treaty establishes Irish Free State with dominion status
1923	Land Act passed by Irish Dail (parliament) completes land purchase

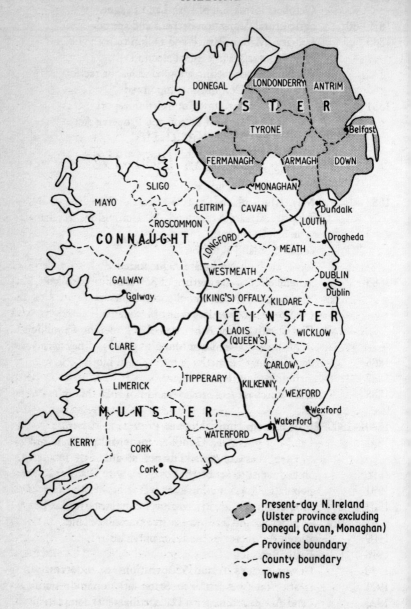

Present-day N. Ireland
(Ulster province excluding
Donegal, Cavan, Monaghan)

——— Province boundary

----- County boundary

• Towns

Ireland and the
Land Question 1800–1922

Interpretations and images

British political control of Ireland can be traced back to a series of military campaigns in the sixteenth and seventeenth centuries. The subjection of the native Irish subsequently relied to a large extent on the collaboration of Protestant settlers from England and Scotland who were granted land and privileges by the British government. In 1782 this Protestant minority's campaign for greater political independence had resulted in the establishment of a Dublin-based legislature, frequently referred to as Grattan's Parliament after its main proponent, Henry Grattan. The limited political autonomy which this enjoyed was short-lived. Full, direct rule from Westminster was reimposed by the Act of Union of 1800 which also allowed Protestant Irish MPs to sit in the British parliament. The alleged consequences of this act and various attempts to modify or repeal it have tended to dominate nineteenth-century Irish history. Only after 1885, however, with Gladstone's commitment to Home Rule, did a significant sector of the British political élite consider conceding any of the demands for greater Irish autonomy. From then on the seemingly increasingly irreconcilable conflict between the interests of the Protestant minority, mainly clustered in Ulster, and those of the rest of the island, has dominated debate. The settlement pieced together between 1920 and 1922 which led to the formation of the Irish Free State resulted in the partition of the island – with six predominantly Protestant counties in north-east Ulster remaining under the protective wing of Westminster.

There is a formidable array of explanations provided by contemporaries and historians to account for Irish refusal to accept British rule. It is difficult to do justice to them in the space available; each is complex, deploys considerable evidence and overlaps with other interpretations. To simplify, however, it is possible to view them as falling into two schools of thought. The former stresses cultural, racial, religious and social factors, the latter alleges that it was British economic exploitation which mobilized opinion.

Until the closing decades of the nineteenth century, however, British politicans overwhelmingly believed that the majority of the Irish could be persuaded to accept permanently the existing political framework of the Union. Various courses of action were pursued, each based on rather different diagnoses of Ireland's problems or needs. The strengthening of the forces of law and order and bouts of vigorous repression were regularly relied on, even favoured in some quarters as the main policy option. As well as deploying the army to maintain public order, the government effected a major reform of the police in the first half of the nineteenth century with the formation of the Peace Preservation Corps in 1814 and the County Constabulary in 1822, later amalgamated in 1836 to create the Irish Constabulary. Coercion Acts were passed during times of social and political unrest and nationalist leaders arrested or, as after the débâcle of the 1916 uprising, executed. Such overt control was supplemented by more subtle attempts to indoctrinate the population and eliminate undesirable social traits. Widespread illiteracy and ignorance, both perceived as causes of backwardness and unruliness, were actively tackled after 1831 through the promotion of a national system of elementary, secular schooling under the National Board of Education. This was designed, in Joseph Lee's words, to obliterate 'subversive ancestral influence by inculcating in the pupils a proper reverence for the English connection, and proper deference for their social superiors'.[1] Official attempts at conversion were supplemented by those of voluntary, usually religious, agencies. Popery itself was frequently regarded, especially by Evangelicals, both as an impediment to social and economic progress and even as explicit evidence of political treachery, since it was claimed that Catholics' first allegiance would always be to a foreign power, the Vatican, and not to the crown. In prefamine Ireland, in particular, there were massive Protestant, and primarily Methodist, missionary endeavours.

Coercion and persuasion were combined with conciliation and concession. Those who believed that religious discrimination was the main grievance, for example, hoped that reform would win the support and confidence of the Catholic clergy and, through them, the laymen, ensuring both social peace and acceptance of British rule. From the late eighteenth century, therefore, restrictions on both the clergy and the laity were removed. Catholics, after 1778, were allowed to own or take out long leases on land. Catholic bishops were reinstated during the following decade. First the vote and then the right to stand for parliament and hold public office were granted by the Catholic Relief Act of 1793 and, amidst considerable controversy, the Catholic Emancipation Act, passed in 1829. A state-aided seminary was established at Maynooth in 1795 to provide Catholic clerical training. The privileges of the Protestant Church of Ireland were swept away by Gladstone's Irish Church Act of 1869.

Amid the profusion of diagnoses and solutions, however, one approach has enjoyed unparalleled support on both sides of the Irish Sea ever since the mid-nineteenth century. This is the view that the key to Ireland's problems lay in the land question. Successive Liberal and Conservative governments, especially after 1870, sought the answer to this 'question of questions for Ireland', as John Devoy, the prominent nationalist and reformer called it, in the hope that it would bring prosperity, peace and acceptance of British rule. Briefly stated, this theory proceeded from the premise that Irish farming was backward and its practitioners poverty-stricken. It then went on to attribute this to the system of land tenure, that is, the conditions under which land was rented to Catholic tenant farmers, conditions which had been introduced by and were allegedly operated for the benefit of Protestant English landlords. Widespread resentment of the system was consequently seen as contributing to Ireland's social unrest, widely reported violence and strident nationalism. From the British point of view, therefore, any lasting political settlement could only be effected if it was accompanied by a solution to the land question. This appealing and popular theory is outlined in more detail below; subsequent chapters will then examine its validity.

Until comparatively recently, few historians questioned the image of Irish rural society which accompanied expositions of the land question. Ireland, in this portrayal, was synonymous with backwardness, poverty, eviction and exploitation. Agriculture was dominated by numerous small farms, all of them inefficiently run. Consequently there was no agricultural revolution to match England's with its enclosures, increasing mechanization, sophisticated land management, manuring, crop rotations and selective breeding of stock. Irish farming remained under-capitalized and the vast majority of the population scraped a pitiful living from tiny plots of land, relying on the ubiquitous, unreliable potato for subsistence. These tenants, generally referred to as peasants, paid extortionate rents to a small number of wealthy, absentee landlords who neglected their duties and siphoned off income from their estates to finance a fine social life in England. Responsibility for Ireland's manifold ills was firmly laid at these landlords' doors. They, it is alleged, helped to sustain rapid population growth before the famine by encouraging the sub-division of holdings which made early marriages possible so that they could expand their rental income. Rather paradoxically, they are also accused of resorting to widespread evictions throughout the century. Consequently, tenant farmers, robbed of capital by extortionate rents and living in perpetual fear of eviction, were unable and unwilling to invest in necessary improvements. The great famine of 1845–9, during which an estimated $1\frac{1}{2}$ to 2 million people fled or starved as potato blight ravaged the countryside, was depicted as the inevitable outcome of landlord, and by implication, British exploitation.

The famine also featured prominently in the history of Irish nationalism. Those who survived the disaster, appalled at apparent British indifference to their plight, were converted *en masse* to the separatist cause. God, so the story goes, may have sent the potato blight but the English caused the famine. The subsequent history of popular nationalism stresses the centrality of the land question especially during the widespread 'Land War' of 1879–82, also popularly portrayed as a rebellion of impoverished peasants against their rich oppressors. More generally, widely reported and seemingly high levels of rural violence or 'agrarian outrages' which made Ireland so difficult to govern were also attributed to disputes about land.

The case for land reform seemed irrefutable to many contemporaries, including members of the British government, when conditions in the province of Ulster were taken into account. Here, although farms were among the smallest in the country (only Connaught in western Ireland possessed a higher proportion of smallholdings), farming seemed to thrive. Visitors commented on the neat white-washed houses, the well-fed, well-dressed inhabitants, the absence of agrarian, as opposed to sectarian violence, and the persistence, even the expansion, of local industry, especially around Belfast. This happy state of affairs was readily attributed to differences in land tenure, specifically the existence of 'Ulster custom' which involved the acceptance and observance of certain unwritten, ill-defined but important tenant rights. Two practices in particular were deemed to be of great significance. First, the tenant farmer in Ulster was assumed to have security of tenure; as long as he paid his rent he could not be evicted and he also had first option on the renewal of any lease when it expired. Second, he could sell his 'interest' in the farm to another, incoming tenant without undue interference on the part of the landlord or could expect, on leaving the farm, to receive payment from the latter for any unexhausted improvements (for example, new buildings, roads, manuring, drainage) which he had undertaken. The combined effect of these rights was to give effective security to farmers, encouraging them, it was argued, to invest in the knowledge that they would not see their rents raised as a result and that they would enjoy the rewards of their efforts. Ulster's experience seemed to offer a solution for the rest of Ireland and, not surprisingly, the extension and formalization of tenant right formed the basis of Gladstone's land acts of 1870 and 1881 (see below, pp. 35–9).

As we shall see, other solutions were also proffered including the abolition of the entire system and its replacement by state ownership or, more commonly, 'peasant' proprietorship where the farmer owned rather than rented the land he tilled. All proceeded, however, from a common diagnosis of the inadequacies of the system of Irish land tenure and the backwardness and poverty of rural society. The land question's contribution to the emergence of strident nationalism also dominated late nineteenth-century political thought and has continued to feature prominently in twentieth-century historical writings. Whether this theory's assumptions were a fair reflection of the reality of Ireland is, therefore, of crucial importance. If they were not, then remedial action based upon them was likely to be at best irrelevant, at worst positively counter-productive, and the traditional view of Irish history seriously misleading.

Realities

INDUSTRY AND POPULATION

'If England has had too much town life,' commented J. L. Hammond, 'Ireland has had too little.'[17] Nineteenth-century Ireland was predominantly a rural country. Only one-fifth of its population of 8.1 million in 1841 lived in towns, generously defined as centres of twenty or more houses. Although this proportion increased fractionally over the century the reasons lay rather in the dramatic decline of rural population than in urban expansion, and many of the smaller towns continued to lose people. By 1901 the Irish population had fallen to 4.5 million. Most settlements were ports or market towns servicing the surrounding countryside, rather than centres of industry. Only Belfast, Dublin and Cork could claim the rank of cities and their expansion, based on a combination of textiles, shipbuilding and commerce, was unexceptional in terms of the British experience, Cork faring least well of the three. In contrast with England, Irish towns were incapable of absorbing surplus rural population.

Eighteenth-century industry, however, had not been confined to towns and rural life had not been synonymous with farming. Domestic or cottage-based manufacturing, especially of textiles, had been widely dispersed throughout Ireland. Although there were concentrations in north Leinster and Ulster, spinning and weaving were carried out all over the country, even transforming Mayo in the far west, a county later devastated by the potato famine of 1845–9, into a thriving centre for the production of linen yarn for export. 'In the closing decades of the century', concludes L. M. Cullen, 'Ireland's economic prospects seemed attractive.'[15] Indeed, from the 1780s English manufacturers were worried that freer trade between the two countries, later brought about by the Act of Union in 1800, would lead to an influx of Irish manufactured goods. Like its counterpart in England, domestic weaving continued to expand in the early years of the nineteenth century. Thereafter, factory-based production, concentrated in south-east Lancashire, the Scottish Lowlands and to a lesser extent north-east Ulster, dealt it a cruel blow from which it never recovered. This collapse of domestic industry robbed small farmers and labourers of a valuable subsidiary source of income. The cause of this industrial failure is still hotly debated but it is most unlikely that the maintenance of protective barriers would have saved Ireland. More important would seem to have been the country's lack of good steam coal; significantly, Belfast on the east coast was able to draw on supplies from west Cumberland and south-west Lancashire.

Ireland's rural problem, therefore, was as much a consequence of this industrial collapse as it was an agricultural crisis. Since there was no organized system of poor relief in Ireland until 1838, this collapse led to an increase in the number of beggars, a feature frequently commented on by visitors to the country, and, for those with some access to land, an increasing dependence on the potato as the means of subsistence. Such employment as existed was now largely restricted to seasonal work on larger farms. For those in the over-populated, barren west of Connaught this necessitated seasonal migration, either to the more commercial eastern counties or to England, where they formed bands of itinerant harvest workers. Those with a specialist skill or sufficient capital fled the country permanently. An estimated 33,000 per annum left for North America in the thirty years before the famine. Even more went to England, settling in the growing factory towns of Lancashire or, more commonly, in the crowded, commercial metropolises of Liverpool and Manchester. Six per cent of Lancashire's entire population in 1841 was Irish, more if the children born to migrants were included. Emigration by that date was running at an estimated 100,000 to 130,000 per annum, the counties of north Leinster, where textiles had once thrived, suffering particularly heavily.

The mass exodus of people during and after the famine of 1845–9 needs to be seen in this context. Industrial stagnation, land shortages, declining agricultural employment and inadequate diet were already combining to choke off population growth by the 1830s. Numbers which had risen by approximately 13 to 14 per cent in each of the first three decades of the century rose by only 5 per cent between 1831 and 1841. There is even some evidence which suggests that absolute numbers had begun to decline by 1845. It would be wrong, therefore, to attribute all the population loss during and after the famine just to the famine. This certainly accelerated the downward trend but any notion that it initiated it is clearly very wide of the mark. Longer-term structural changes in the economy were more important influences.

We should not assume, however, that those who left the country, or the minority who resided in urban areas, can safely be written out of any discussion of Irish social or political problems and protests, even those which appear to have been specifically about rural concerns. The prosperity of most towns was inextricably linked with that of the surrounding farming communities and, as we shall see, their inhabitants, especially artisans, shopkeepers and commercial and professional men, often took active roles in land agitation and wider political movements. Much individual and financial support also came from the Irish overseas.

AGRICULTURE

Although there were marked regional variations and considerable hardship for much of the population, especially in the second quarter of the nineteenth century, Irish agriculture was relatively successful in adapting to changing market conditions and more and more farmers enjoyed increasing prosperity, especially after 1850.

Eighteenth-century farming was already finely tuned to the needs of the English market. Since Ireland enjoyed a 'maritime climate' with mild winters and plentiful rain, grass grew luxuriantly for much of the year and farmers were ideally placed to specialize in livestock and dairy husbandry. Traditionally, live cattle had comprised the bulk of the exports, but from the 1760s with corn shortages and rising prices in England brought about by her expanding population, farmers increasingly put their pastures under the plough to grow corn. The disruption caused to European supplies during the long French wars after 1793 accelerated this development. This switch to arable farming encouraged both the reclamation of previously uncultivated waste land and the cultivation of potatoes both as part of a regular crop rotation and as a way of breaking in the newly reclaimed ground. The increased workforce required for labour-intensive arable farming were paid partly in kind in the form of potato plots. These developments, coupled with the buoyancy of domestic industry, undoubtedly contributed to the noticeable quickening in the rate of growth of the population from the late eighteenth century.

Although it is still common practice to portray the famine as the important turning-point in Irish agricultural history, many historians have followed R. D. Crotty's pioneering work, *Irish Agricultural Production*,[7] in arguing that the move away from such arable farming actually began rather earlier, possibly in 1815, more plausibly from the mid-1830s. As with demographic changes, the famine accelerated rather than initiated trends. Grain prices collapsed after the Napoleonic wars, causing deep depression and distress on both sides of the Irish Sea. Prices for livestock products dropped less spectacularly, however, and this, combined with Ireland's climatic advantages and the development of steamship services which were quicker and more reliable than those operated by sailing vessels, encouraged farmers to switch back to pasture. As in England, this shift took several decades to effect, corn exports continuing to rise until the mid-1830s, but evidence that pastoral farming revived seems irrefutable. Live-cattle exports rose from just under 47,000 animals per year between 1821 and 1825, to over 98,000 in 1835 and an average of 190,800 per year between 1846 and 1848 at the height of the famine. Sheep exports doubled over the same period.

Although this brought prosperity to those larger farmers engaged in the trade it worsened the lot of the majority of the population. Pastoral farming required few labourers. Coupled with the collapse of domestic industry, the decline in demand for labour proved disastrous for the smallholders and labourers. Dependence on the potato increased alarmingly, especially in the west where inferior land, poor communications and distance from ports restricted both the development of commercial farming and the prospects of emigrating. Periodic famine was endemic as the potato crops failed or proved inadequate to support families through the winter. Social tension in the countryside escalated with the prospect of clearance and eviction to make way for larger pastoral farms. The widespread destruction of the famine which wiped out upwards of $1\frac{1}{2}$ million impoverished smallholders and labourers or forced them to flee overseas, speeded up and consolidated the expansion of commercial pastoral farming.

For nearly thirty years after the famine, with only one noticeable depression in fortunes between 1859 and 1864, Irish farming and farmers prospered. Price trends coupled with an expansion of the rail network continued to favour livestock and dairy farming. The quality of animals improved dramatically as new breeds were introduced and, while the number of cattle rose by 60 per cent in the half-century after 1850, sheep flocks doubled. The annual average value of agricultural output (excluding potatoes) rose by 40 per cent from £28.8 million between 1851 and 1855 to £40.64 million between 1871 and 1875. Farmers' incomes increased by an estimated 77 per cent over the same period while bank deposits increased fourfold from £8 million in 1845 to £33 million in 1876. As a result of this increased spending power, shops spread rapidly throughout Ireland, even in the far west where their absence during the famine had proved so disastrous for government attempts to relieve distress through market channels. In contrast with pre-famine years, the population fell steadily throughout this period creating occasional labour shortages which marginally pushed up the daily wage rate by the 1860s. Even smallholders in the west – where farming remained less developed, potatoes retained their importance as a staple crop and the population was beginning to rise again by the 1860s – enjoyed a modest prosperity as the cattle which they sold to pay the rent went up in value and seasonal earnings for harvest work in the east or in England remained buoyant.

A more prolonged depression set in from the late 1870s. Farmers' reaction to this downturn in fortunes was swift and purposeful (see pp. 27–9), although it was far less serious than that which devastated

9

less responsive English arable farmers. The influx of American grain after 1877 which slashed the English market price had less impact in Ireland where corn accounted for perhaps only 10 per cent of gross agricultural output. Imports into Britain of cheap but inferior chilled and frozen meat, which expanded in the 1880s, had less effect on the demand for, and price of, good quality Irish produce. The crisis arose rather from domestic difficulties. In the west the potato crop failed successively for several years after 1877. This, combined with reduced opportunities for emigration to North America and the decline of seasonal employment in fishing or harvesting, pushed smallholders there to the brink of disaster, decimating their pig and poultry numbers, ending thirty years of comparative prosperity. Falling prices for butter, combined with exceptionally inclement weather which encouraged the spread of disease among farm stock and laid low hay crops, hit more substantial farmers all over Ireland. Conditions improved from the mid-1880s and by 1890 farmers' profitability had been restored assisted by the judicially fixed 'fair' rents which followed Gladstone's Land Act of 1881 (see pp. 38–9). Stability and relative prosperity characterized the late Victorian and Edwardian decades with bank deposits, a reliable indicator of national wealth, doubling between 1890 and 1914.

This generally favourable picture is not intended to minimize the disaster of the famine for the Irish people. Nor does it necessarily invalidate criticisms of the inefficiency of Irish farming and its possible failure to reach full potential. But it does have several important implications for our study. First, it is clear that agriculture, especially after the famine and at the time that British politicians began to take an active interest in the land question, was neither as backward nor as poverty-stricken as is sometimes imagined. It was commercially orientated and its practitioners were better able to ride out adverse corn price movements than the highly capitalized, dangerously vulnerable, southern English farmers. Second, marked regional variations persisted throughout the century. Connaught and parts of west Munster remained less developed, with a significantly higher percentage of smallholders who, despite the heavy mortality of the famine years, when over 25 per cent perished, and the small improvement in conditions which followed, continued to rely heavily on a potato diet. Subsequent population loss here was less dramatic than in other regions and it was not until the last two decades of the century that sustained emigration emerged. Leinster and east Munster were to the forefront of the move to pastoral farming and, even before the famine, contained a higher percentage of larger farmers. Finally, this re-appraisal demands a re-interpretation of land-lord-tenant relations and the nature, extent and timing of Irish social and political protest.

LANDOWNERS

Until the turn of this century the greater part of the land in Ireland (97 per cent in 1870) was owned by men who rented it out to tenant farmers rather than cultivating it themselves. A clear, unequivocal image of these landlords as large, rich, English, Protestant absentees pervades many of the histories written in the first half of the twentieth century. How accurate is it?

As in England, the individual wealth of members of the landowning class varied considerably, depending on the size, quality and location of properties. Smaller landlords in the east, in Ulster or on the outskirts of towns were more favourably placed than the owners of tracts of infertile bog in the west. Precise information on both the pattern of landowner-ship and individual estates in the first half of the nineteenth century is remarkably patchy. There were probably less than 10,000 proprietors of 100 or more acres in 1830 but this number includes many who owned relatively small estates and a few aristocratic magnates. More precise official statistics are available for 1870 and these confirm the view that diversity rather than uniformity characterized the landlord class. A mere 302 proprietors, 1.5 per cent of the total, possessed 33.7 per cent of the land and 50 per cent of the country was in the hands of 750 families. At the other end of the scale, 15,527, or 80.5 per cent, owned between them only 19.3 per cent of the land. Some historians have suggested that, since these smaller landlords were less likely to be able to spread their risks or to rely substantially on income from other investments, they were more likely to raise rents than their larger counterparts, but there is no precise evidence to support any clear correlation between size and attitudes to estate management.

Absenteeism, the practice of residing elsewhere than on one's estate, is also commonly accepted to have been a universal practice in Ireland and detrimental to the country's progress. Its existence cannot be denied but both its alleged universality and its supposedly unfavourable consequences can be queried. Although it has been less commented on or studied, absenteeism was prevalent in England too. Large tracts of the north of England were devoid of resident landowners. In parts of Lincolnshire in the mid-nineteenth century only 7 per cent of parishes

11

had permanently resident substantial landowners. Throughout the United Kingdom, parliamentary politics, involvement in the armed forces or civil service, sport, investment concerns and the management of scattered portions of their estates frequently resulted in long absences from home. Before the famine an estimated one-third to one-half of Irish landlords were absentees but in 1870 only 13.3 per cent, owning 23 per cent of the land, were permanently resident outside the country. Internal absentees, that is landlords who resided elsewhere in Ireland than on their estate, accounted for 36.6 per cent of the total, but half of the country was owned by men who resided on or near their property. Absenteeism, however, did not necessarily bring about inefficient estate management or rack-renting, the charging of excessively high rents. The majority of substantial proprietors employed estate agents to manage their affairs. When, as was sometimes the case, these men's enthusiasm for efficiency, maximization of rental income or both overcame their caution or humanity, aggrieved tenants could turn to the absentee as an appeal judge. Permanent absentees, however, were usually the larger and possibly more financially secure landowners who may have had less cause to raise rents and more funds to improve their estates. Significantly, some of the most infamous landlords who experienced the full force of tenant opposition during the Land War crisis of 1879–82 were permanently resident on their estates. The fiercest critics of absentees for much of the century, however, were not farmers but resident landlords who felt that they were unfairly expected to shoulder unpalatable, time-consuming, local, social and political responsibilities for which they received no pecuniary reward and scant recognition. As Samuel Clark has recently commented, 'One cannot assume . . . that resident landlords had better relations with their tenantry, or even that absenteeism had much effect one way or the other on landlord-tenant relationships.'[6]

Although substantially correct, the view that Irish land was owned exclusively by English Protestants or by families with strong personal and material connections with England also needs to be qualified, especially for the late nineteenth century. During the sixteenth and seventeenth centuries the British government had confiscated all Catholics' lands and enacted penal laws restricting landownership to Protestants. Although these acts had been repealed in 1778, few Catholics purchased land before the famine. Those who succeeded in trade or business, primarily in the eastern seaboard towns, discovered, like their middle-class counterparts in England, that complete estates were still beyond their reach and that existing proprietors were unwilling to sell off land piecemeal and guarded the integrity of their estates with complicated familial and legal arrangements. Such legal restraints were lifted by the Encumbered Estates Act of 1849 making the sale of land less complicated and costly. By 1870 a substantial minority of landlords, 40 per cent according to one estimate, were Catholics. Their estates, however, seem to have been generally smaller than those of the Protestants and because of this and the decline in subletting which had been practised by Catholic middlemen before the famine (see pp. 15–16), it is probable that the proportion of tenant farmers who rented their land directly from Protestant landowners actually increased over the century and consequently social divisions continued to mirror religious distinctions.

One of the most significant, but, until recently, one of the least recognized features of this class needs to be borne in mind because it helps to explain both its members' attitudes to estate management and, from the 1880s, their willingness and need to sell out. Almost without exception landowners were in debt. In this they were no different from their English counterparts. Since expenditure on family settlements, lavish establishments and lifestyles or, in some cases, agricultural improvement, tended to outstrip income from rents and investments, they borrowed on the security of their property. Loans were not difficult to raise. Creditors were happy to do business with men who could offer something as solid as land as guarantee that their debts could be repaid. For many of them, for much of the century, indebtedness was not an indication of imminent financial collapse or a matter which unduly worried them. Lord Downshire, one of the few large landowners whose estate papers have been scrutinized, borrowed £186,500 between 1810 and 1840, apparently without straining his resources or his creditors' goodwill. However, some who had borrowed heavily during the Napoleonic wars, when interest rates were high, began to find it difficult to maintain repayments in the difficult years of transition to pastoral farming which followed when small, uneconomic arable farmers fell progressively behind with their rents. During the great famine landlords' incomes plummeted as thousands of small tenants defaulted on their rent. This was accompanied by a huge rise in outgoings. The system of poor relief introduced into Ireland in 1838 was financed out of local rates, a tax levied on occupiers of property. The poor themselves, however, were exempted from paying this if the property they inhabited was valued at less than £4 per annum for rental purposes; their landlords were committed to paying their rates. The massive cost of relieving the widespread destitution after 1845, therefore, had to be borne by landlords. In an attempt to reduce the number of paupers in areas for which they were responsible, landlords resorted to evictions, the tragic consequences of which are well known. Even this ruthless policy was not sufficient to rescue many landowners from financial ruin and bankruptcy. After the Encumbered Estates Act of 1849 simplified the processes of buying and selling land, many grasped the opportunity to sell out. Over one-third of Ireland changed hands under its terms in the decade which followed.

The problem of landlord indebtedness was further increased by the unfavourable economic climate of the late 1870s and early 1880s and by Gladstone's legislation if 1881 which removed their power to fix rent levels (see pp. 37–8). With land values falling, loans were difficult to raise, while falling rent rolls reduced income dramatically. Landowners accustomed to devoting 20 to 25 per cent of their incomes to servicing debts now found repayments accounted for 40 per cent or more. The Earl of Lucan, with large tracts of land in Mayo, devoted a staggering 85 per cent to this purpose by 1905. Such financial considerations obviously influenced the policies which landlords adopted towards their tenants and towards schemes to encourage owner-occupancy (see pp. 39–41).

TENANTS

It is commonplace to portray Ireland as a country of peasants, poor subsistence farmers eking out a precarious existence on small patches of land, generally planted with potatoes, and uninvolved in the market economy except in so far as they were obliged to pay rent to landlords and taxes to Church and state. In reality rural society was far more complex than this with no clear distinctions between classes and significant variations between regions and over time.

The majority of the population in pre-famine Ireland had little or no access to land. They lived in appalling conditions. Forty per cent of Irish houses in 1841 were one room, mud cabins with natural earth floors, no windows and no chimneys. Furniture and cooking facilities in these hovels were equally primitive. Their inhabitants' diet was both monotonous and increasingly inadequate. Beggars and paupers apart, virtually landless labourers, or cottiers, occupied the lowest rung on the social ladder. The 596,000 returned in the census of 1841 comprised the largest single occupational or social group in the country. These people faced a shrinking demand for their services after the Napoleonic wars as domestic industry declined and corn growing contracted. The more fortunate, usually young single men, were engaged as farm servants, boarding with their employer and receiving a small cash wage. The casually employed fared less well. Before 1838 in the absence of a system of poor relief, such as existed in England to tide labourers over the winter months, irregularly employed married men relied on small potato plots for survival. These were often rented on a yearly basis from local farmers and paid for by labour services, a system known as conacre.

The distinction between these cottiers and the 408,000 smallholders listed in the census returns was a blurred one. The very smallest, some 65,000 with holdings of one acre or less, were virtually indistinguishable from them and even those with a few acres more had to rely on extra income from elsewhere or access to so-called waste for common grazing and peat-digging. Some combined small-scale tillage with a trade but the majority depended on casual earnings in the ailing domestic industries, collecting kelp (seaweed used for fertilizer or the production of alkali) and fishing on the west coast, and seasonal work on larger farms during harvest, this last increasingly necessitating journeys to England. Smallholders with between 6 and 15 acres might more correctly be regarded as small farmers, possessing, on average, two cows and a horse and employing one or two farm servants. Whatever their size, virtually none had written agreements with their landlords to give them legal security of tenure. An unspecified number, which probably increased in the first half of the century, were squatters who had no recognized right at all to the land which they occupied.

The sad plight of these groups dominates contemporary and much historical writing but they did not constitute the entire population and both their numbers and economic significance declined dramatically from the mid-century. Once again, distinctions are blurred, but a further 453,000 individuals were returned in 1841 as farmers. Some of these, especially graziers, were clearly significantly larger than the smallholders and ranked as men of some standing and wealth. They enjoyed a comfortable standard of living, participated in local and national politics, supported and financed the Catholic Church, arranged financially beneficial marriages and careers for their offspring and even provided social leadership in the absence of local landowners. In a significant number of instances they were also landlords to the smallholders and cottiers, subletting land which they rented on long leases from the landowner. The extent of this practice remains unclear. Such middlemen, as they were called, undoubtedly flourished in the era of corn growing, when they had an obvious interest in increasing the numbers of labourers for their farms. Some historians have argued that the system declined rapidly in the 1820s but regional studies have shown that it survived up to, and possibly beyond, the famine. J. S. Donnelly's examination of the county of Cork[16] includes reference to one farm let to a family in 1770 which had over 300 inhabitants by 1845, most of them sub-tenants of the original leaseholder. In 1843 there were 12,529 tenants on the Trinity College estate, but only one per cent of these paid their rent to the college, 45 per cent were sub-tenants of this small number and over 52 per cent were sub-tenants of these sub-tenants.

Throughout the century, Connaught and Ulster had much higher proportions of smallholders in their populations than the other two provinces. In the west, with its infertile terrain and unreliable communications, conditions closely matched the popular image of peasant Ireland and the marked distinction between the experiences here and those in the rest of the country have led some historians to talk of a 'dual economy'. Commercial farming made more progress elsewhere. The smallholders of Ulster found ready markets for their produce in the expanding towns of the north-east which also absorbed any surplus rural population and thus helped to maintain living standards on the land. Leinster and Munster, where pastoral farming made most headway before the famine, had more substantial farmers, the small tenants here being increasingly forced on to less hospitable land. The passage of time reinforced rather than eroded these regional differences. Despite the catastrophe of 1845–9, a smallholding economy persisted in the west. The social structure there remained largely unchanged for another thirty years although the dire poverty was relieved somewhat by the buoyant market for agricultural produce and the reduction in population. More substantial pastoral farmers increasingly dominated the society, and the politics, of the south and east of the country. By the 1850s, although small farmers were still numerically preponderant, most of Ireland was organized into large farms. One estimate for 1854 calculated that 74 per cent of farmers (including smallholders) had fewer than 30 acres but that those with 50 acres or more occupied 60 per cent of the land. The prosperity and progress of Irish agriculture increasingly depended not so much on the smallholding class but on this comfortable, educated, self-confident rural bourgeoisie.

The role of the famine in bringing about this revolution in social structure is not in dispute. Hundreds of thousands of cottiers and small-holders who had increasingly relied on a subsistence potato diet died of starvation and disease or were forced to flee the country. Historians, however, are increasingly unwilling to accept that this tragedy was also a turning-point. First, they point to the survival of the smallholding economy in the west. Second, they stress that, as with demographic and agricultural trends, the famine acted as an accelerator rather than an initiator. The poorer classes, who were the fiercest opponents of the amalgamation and consolidation of holdings into larger farms, certainly suffered between 1845 and 1851 but they had already been losing ground to larger pastoral farmers, espcially in Leinster and Munster, before the famine. Third, historians now accept P. M. A. Bourke's statistical revision of the precise impact of the famine on farm structure.[13] In an important article in 1965, he considerably reduced the previously accepted figures, based on a comparison of the 1841 and 1851 censuses, of the number of holdings which disappeared. The 1841 figures referred to Irish acres which are approximately three-fifths as large again as their English counterparts. Ten years later census enumerators were instructed to make their returns in English acres and also to include 'waste' and land occupied by the farm buildings themselves as part of the holdings. The two sets of figures, therefore, are not comparable. Measured in English acres, farms were in fact much larger before the famine than 1841 material suggests. Changes in landholding patterns were 'both less sensational and more credible' than has traditionally been argued.

LANDLORD-TENANT RELATIONSHIPS

The preceding survey of agricultural and social trends clearly has major implications for any study of the land question and particularly for landlord-tenant relations which are widely regarded as a central element of the problem. Dealings between these groups are generally assumed to have been far from cordial or conducive to good farming practices and, after the famine, mounting pressure persuaded the government to intervene in the field.

Until recently there seemed little doubt as to which party was responsible for the unsatisfactory state of affairs. Anti-landlord propaganda which portrayed tenants as powerless victims of landlord oppression has been a major influence on both political and historical approaches to the subject. Landlordism, according to Michael Davitt, the Fenian leader,

17

(see p. 28), writing at the time of the Land War of 1879–82, was a 'foul, pestiferous, social rinderpest'. The landlords themselves were 'a brood of cormorant vampires that has sucked the life blood out of the country'. His colleague, John Devoy, echoed his views: 'The landlord system is the greatest curse inflicted by England on Ireland, and Ireland will never be prosperous or happy until it is rooted out.' Landlords have traditionally been found guilty of several related crimes against the Irish tenants. The rents they charged have generally been considered to have been excessively high, bordering on legalized robbery. Even if their tenants paid these extortionate rents they are reputed to have lived under permanent threat of eviction, without notice or reason, since landlords regularly resorted to widespread and indiscriminate clearances. Such practices were not only morally indefensible but also economically ruinous, starving the countryside of capital, eroding tenant farmers' incentive to invest. Ireland's poverty, even the famine itself was, therefore, the ultimate responsibility of the landowning class. The landlords' defence received short shrift in the nineteenth century and only recently have historians begun to piece together a plausible alternative version of events which portrays them in a more sympathetic light.

The landlords' indifference, even antagonism towards agricultural improvement, is alleged to have manifested itself, particularly before the famine, in the encouragement they gave to the proliferation of uneconomic smallholdings which promised to expand their rental income. It now seems more likely that it was the larger, arable tenant farmers who, as middlemen, encouraged such sub-division to expand their labour supply during the boom years of the Napoleonic wars. In contrast, landlords tended to view the formation of substantial pastoral holdings favourably by the 1820s since these were economically viable and promised a secure return. Landlords' failure to invest significant amounts in improving their estates, even when farming profitability was rising dramatically in mid-century is also a long-standing criticism partially vindicated by recent research carried out by W. E. Vaughan.[12] Whether heavy capital outlay was desirable, or even possible, however, is far from clear. In England in the 1850s, capital-intensive 'high farming' was generally confined to arable areas and was ultimately unprofitable, its enthusiastic supporters tending to confuse technical efficiency with economic rationality. Pastoral farming offered less scope for such investment, especially in Ireland, where the milder climate reduced the need for winter accommodation for livestock. Investment was further

18

restricted by landlords' indebtedness and the persistence in some areas of small-scale, uneconomic holdings, but certain landlords do appear to have been active in the relatively cheap, yet vitally important, area of improving livestock breeds. Possibly the major consequence of limited capital investment was a social rather than an economic one. By making financial transactions between tenant and landlord one-directional, it bestowed credibility on the image of the landlord as a non-productive parasite.

Alleged mistreatment of tenants is a more serious charge. Precise information on the level of evictions in the first half of the century is not available. They were certainly not frequent occurrences until after 1815 and even then many were probably carried out, not by landowners, but by the larger tenant farmers who had sub-let their holdings. When the owners dealt directly with small tenants they often found it difficult or distasteful to resort to massive evictions. Concerned landlords realized that, in the absence of alternative employment, those deprived of access to land would have no means of survival. Some, therefore, offered dispossessed tenants free or subsidized passages to North America or attempted to foster local industries. Others simply chose to try to check any further sub-division of holdings or waited until these fell vacant before amalgamating them to form larger farms. Yet others were doubtless prevented from acting by sustained violent, collective protest by their intended victims (see pp. 22–3). Although amalgamation and consolidation of farms was evident, therefore, the wholesale clearances and forced evictions which occurred in the Scottish highlands at this time were not repeated in Ireland. During the famine years, however, when all hope of collecting rent arrears had vanished and landowners' poor-rate payments were escalating, and during the Land War of 1879–82, when tenants collectively withheld payment of rent, evictions were common in Ireland. At other times the widely reported threats of ejectment were intended to be, and were generally accepted as, final demands for payment and were treated as such. Few were translated into actual evictions. After the famine these were rare, averaging only 1.36 per 1000 holdings per year between 1854 and 1880. They were particularly low in Connaught despite the high proportion of smallholders there. Consequently, although many tenants, like those in England, did not have legally binding, written agreements with their landlords which guaranteed their security of tenure, most came to expect to be able to retain possession of their farms so long as they paid their rents. The legislation of 1870 and 1881, therefore, effectively gave legal backing to practices which already existed. It is now also becoming increasingly clear that a minority of farmers, usually the substantial graziers, did have written leases which guaranteed their security for several decades. The economic historian, J. Mokyr, has recently estimated that these large leaseholders farmed as much as 75 per cent of Irish land as early as 1854.[10] Any interpretation of the land question that attributes alleged Irish backwardness to insecurity of tenure or evictions is falsely grounded. One that argues that these features were the cause of social and political unrest is primarily applicable to the activities of the smallholding and cottier classes in pre-famine decades.

Whether tenants were charged extortionate rents for this security or whether all landowners have been damned because of the widely publicized rack-renting of a few of their number whose infamy was originally based on the fact that they were the exceptions to the rule, remains to be examined. The concept of an extortionate rent is of course a subjective one. Statistical tables of gross rents or charges per acre signify nothing unless they are related to the quality of the land, size of holding, market conditions and general ability to pay. The impoverished small-holders and cottiers of pre-famine Ireland, many of whom paid their rent to middlemen rather than directly to landowners, would still have struggled had they had to pay nothing for their land. Even a few pounds a year could be crippling. Larger pastoral farmers encountered little difficulty in paying economic rents for their holdings. Although rents had gone up in line with agricultural prices during the boom years before 1815, there is no evidence to suggest that landowners endeavoured to expropriate a higher share of the profits or that in subsequent decades they deliberately fixed rents to pauperize their tenants. Rents were not the major cause of social unrest during these years.

Although some farmers faced increases of 40 per cent in the generally prosperous years between 1850 and the Land League's morally indignant call for 'fair rents' in the early 1880s, the majority of landlords failed to exploit their estates fully and allowed rents to stagnate or fall below the real letting value of the land. Evidence that tenants refrained from investing because they feared that punitive rent increases would follow, or that extortionate rents choked off funds for investment, is singularly lacking. Rents were raised only rarely, if at all, usually at the expiration of a lease or at infrequent general revaluations of estates, while rent abatements were often conceded in the occasional depressed year. Such practices ensured that, as in England and Scotland, rents lagged behind price rises of agricultural produce and farmers' profits increased from mid-century onwards.

The failure to charge competitive rents is probably more correctly attributed to unadventurous landlord policies than to the strength of any tenant opposition. Faced with irreducible outgoings to service their debts and family commitments (see pp. 13–14), the landowners were wary about raising rents if there was the remotest possibility that this could increase the chances of non-payment. They preferred a guaranteed, regular income to short-term maximization of profits, hoping that by this they would also retain the goodwill of their tenants. The results of the policy, however, were far from satisfactory, at least from their point of view. First and almost paradoxically, low rents may have retarded economic progress by inflating farmers' profits, encouraging complacency and reducing their need to become more competitive to remain in business. Second, since landlords failed to capitalize on the rising market of the mid-Victorian years, they were poorly placed to cope with the demand for yet lower rents which accompanied the slump in agricultural fortunes after 1877. Third, inexplicable and illogical increases and variations in rent levels undoubtedly created resentment among farmers who complained about the inequity of the system. Notions of what constituted a 'fair rent' were arrived at by comparison with neighbours rather than by reference to market trends. Simply because they were infrequent and unpredictable, any rises in rents were likely to be viewed as 'unfair'. Finally, increasingly prosperous farmers developed a further reason for preventing rents rising towards their true, competitive market value. Increases, especially those imposed at the end of leases, had the undesirable effect, from the farmers' point of view, of reducing the value of any tenant rights which they enjoyed. Potential purchasers of leasehold farms were clearly only willing to pay outgoing tenants for the privilege of possession if they considered that the rentals were low. The higher the rent, therefore, the lower the marketable value of any tenant rights. Not surprisingly farmers increasingly campaigned not only for the legal recognition of tenant rights, but also for restrictions on the ability of landlords to raise rents.

OVERVIEW

Conditions in Ireland, then, were rather different from those which many contemporaries and later historians have portrayed. While it is impossible to refute the findings of such detailed official enquiries as the Devonshire Commission of 1844 which stressed the poverty and misery of the majority of the Irish people, it would be wrong to assume that all of the population suffered or that conditions remained unchanged in subsequent decades. Landlord policies can be partly vindicated and logically explained. The tenant farmers for whom Gladstone sought justice after 1870 were far from exploited or impoverished. Why, then, was Ireland considered, in Gladstone's words, to be in need of 'pacification' by 1868? What precisely was the land question which dominated debate? Was it really the cause of Ireland's social discontent and the driving force behind the burgeoning nationalist movement?

Social unrest and political mobilization

AGRARIAN OUTRAGES AND RURAL VIOLENCE

Rural Ireland and its apparent endemic violence has received far more attention than the English countryside despite the fact that this, too, was far from an untroubled society, with major outbreaks of collective protest in the southern and eastern counties in 1816 and 1830–1 and persistent, often malicious crimes against persons and property. Although there are numerous examples of Irish unrest before the famine, precise figures are not available until the police began to compile detailed records from the mid-1830s. From 1844 a separate record of 'agrarian outrages' was compiled, although the criteria for distinguishing these from other rural crimes always remained obscure. Homicides – legitimized in some eyes as 'assassinations' – assaults and other 'offences against the person' attracted the most concern but formed only a small proportion of total outrages. More common were injuries to property – chiefly incendiarism and the maiming of animals – and general 'offences against the public peace', predominantly the sending of threatening letters. Although such crimes were to be found in England, they were usually the work of individuals acting independently; in Ireland they were generally perpetrated by sinister secret societies. These underground, locally based organizations seem to have enjoyed the complete loyalty which they demanded among significant sections of the rural community. Their exotic names – Shaunavests, Terry Alts, Rockites, Blackfeet, Molly Maguires, Whitefeet, Whiteboys – ritual initiation ceremonies and oath-taking, further alarmed the authorities.

The first outbreaks of Whiteboyism, a term which is commonly used to cover the activities of all such societies, occurred in the 1760s but activity and concern seem to have peaked as population pressures mounted during the 1820s and 1830s. Participants were invariably drawn from the poorer strata of society, not the completely destitute or landless, but the smallholding and cottier classes. The rural disturbances, however, were not equally prevalent throughout the country. In Connaught and Ulster, where smallholders were most numerous, outrages were less frequent than in the more commercially orientated, advanced provinces of Leinster and Munster. Within this region there were frequent sporadic outbursts of collective activity. From the mid-1830s to the famine, Tipperary enjoyed the dubious distinction of being considered the most violent county, but no one area retained its lead for long and all were affected at some stage. This suggests that unrest was not simply a natural consequence of a backward, poverty-stricken peasant society but a response to deliberately engineered changes which threatened the foundations of that society.

Unravelling the motives of these societies' members, however, is far from easy. A few historians have suggested that their activities reflected the high spirits of the under-employed, adolescent age group, a large proportion of society during a period of population growth. Others have stressed the possibility of frequent family quarrels, especially over inheritances, which were bound to occur when access to land was so vital for survival. The recourse to collective intimidation by labourers and cottiers to assist negotiations with farmers over wages or conacre holdings cannot be ruled out; nor can the possibility of tenants' concern over rent levels. But a more basic conflict over the actual access to land seems to be the most feasible and widely accepted explanation. Significantly the most violent counties were those where large-scale, pastoral farming was making most headway. Here, smallholders and cottiers, threatened with clearance or resettlement and faced with the prospect of declining employment opportunities, resisted the necessary amalgamation and consolidation of farms which such commercial agriculture was deemed to require. Although landlords responsible for pursuing such a policy were often targets, tenant farmers who collaborated with them, enhancing their wealth and status at the expense of their neighbours, were also severely dealt with.

It is important to recognize that this conflict over land in pre-famine Ireland was largely devoid of sectarian or nationalist overtones. Although disputes often reflected the Protestant-Catholic divide, the underlying causes were invariably economic and Catholic tenant farmers deemed to have transgressed in the eyes of the poorer classes were meted out the same treatment. Far from supporting such activity, the Catholic clergy condemned it and sought to arbitrate or find peaceful solutions to problems. Their intervention occasionally earned them communal displeasure, driving a wedge between the Church and the majority of the people. Only on the Ulster borders, especially in Armagh, was open sectarian warfare waged from as early as the 1780s between the Protestant Peep O'Day Boys and the Catholic Defenders, respective forerunners of the Orange Order and Ribbonism. This latter movement enjoyed fluctuating popularity in the early nineteenth century as a lower-class organization with nationalist overtones, peaking between 1815 and 1822 and gaining support in the Dublin area during these years. Its hold over the rural population, however, was never strong. Its leaders and followers were generally drawn from the urban commercial and trading classes – shopkeepers, artisans, publicans, even schoolteachers – and it was largely absent in areas where Whiteboyism was strong.

The famine, by wiping out a significant portion of the smallholding class, effectively curtailed wholesale rural protest and agrarian outrages. Official statistics show a marked decline in the number of agrarian outrages as the famine deepened during 1846 and 1847 but a significant increase in petty theft, the product of individual desperation rather than collective resistance. Between 1854 and 1878 outrages averaged only 305 per year, or 55 for every 100,000 holdings over one acre, while homicides never exceeded 11 and rarely rose above 5 per year. Only in 1870 and between 1879 and 1882 did numbers rise temporarily, in the first instance because the police briefly changed the criteria for the collection of the statistics, in the latter as a response to evictions during the Land War (see pp. 28–32). 'In political and social terms the Famine quite clearly resolved the conflict between the interests of the poorer peasantry and those of the commercially minded rural classes firmly in favour of the latter', concludes Michael Beames. 'The prospect of some major political change in Ireland based on a mass movement of impoverished peasants was swept away by the Famine.'[4]

POLITICAL MOBILIZATION

The organizations which feature so prominently in political histories of nineteenth-century Irish nationalism were much more sophisticated than the local societies which fought over the land and they did not rely for their support on the poorer social classes.

Daniel O'Connell's Catholic Association was formed in 1823 to campaign by constitutional methods for Catholic emancipation, that is, for the right of Catholics to hold public office and stand for election to the British parliament. Although it attempted to mobilize the lower classes through the introduction of penny subscriptions in 1824 it relied on the clergy for its national organization and the larger farmers and urban middle classes for its regular support and finance. The so-called forty shilling 'freeholders' on whom its electoral success depended in the 1820s, far from being the poorest sections of society, were either owner-occupiers or leaseholders who were prepared to swear publicly that their farms were worth at least forty shillings more per year than the amounts which they paid to their landlords thus giving them an 'interest' in the holding. S. J. Connolly's recent scholarly examination of the pre-famine Church[14] has also emphasized that it was these wealthier elements in rural society which supported the Catholic ministry. Both O'Connell's and the Catholic Church's hold over the majority of the Irish population in these decades were always weak. Smallholders and cottiers had little reason to welcome the Catholic Emancipation Act which was passed in 1829; it offered no solution to the conflict over land and gave political and social recognition to some of their opponents, the larger Catholic graziers. Indeed, O'Connell's prescription for a prosperous Ireland was an expansion of large-scale, commercial, pastoral farming and he openly criticized the struggle of secret agrarian societies who were opposed to this.

The Tithe War of the 1830s also drew disproportionate support from larger tenant farmers. The payment of tithe, essentially a legally binding, ecclesiastical tax on land payable to the Protestant Church of Ireland, had long been a source of grievance, but a package of reforms introduced in 1823 had shifted the burden from the smaller arable farmer to the livestock specialist by abolishing the previous exemption which grassland had enjoyed. Although secret societies remained concerned about the tax, the national campaign, which was ultimately successful in effecting a reform of the methods of assessment and collection in 1838, was dominated by wealthy graziers and large farmers.

After the success of Catholic Emancipation, O'Connell turned his attention to effecting a repeal of the Act of Union of 1800 which had abolished the semi-autonomous Irish parliament. His Society for the Repeal of the Union was launched in 1830 but it was not until 1841 that he sought to broaden the base of public support through a Repeal Association. Well attended 'monster meetings' in market towns during the summer months certainly worried the government but the platform was invariably dominated by landowners, and the crowd's motivation for attending is far from clear, one historian, G. Ó Tuathaigh, describing the atmosphere as 'a mixture of fair, football game and evangelical revival'.[1] A number of landowners, both Protestant and Catholic, were staunch supporters, along with some larger farmers, but Ireland's small urban population was again over-represented and the largely peasant society of the west showed little interest in the movement.

When the British government showed itself unwilling to concede to O'Connell's constitutional movement, Young Ireland, a breakaway intellectual faction, began to call for more militant action in their newspaper, the *Nation*. Its leading figures were young, Protestant intellectuals in Dublin and its appeal remained largely urban. Far from mobilizing nationalist support for either O'Connell or the Young Irelanders, the famine contributed to their demise. Fired by the revolutions on the continent, Young Irelanders planned an uprising in 1848. Despite their championing of a complete overhaul of the land system in favour of the smallholders, it was poorly supported in the famine-ravaged countryside; the daily search for food seemed far more important than idealistic hopes of independence.

The tendency for overt nationalism to rely primarily on the towns continued through the prosperous post-famine decades up to the late 1870s. The Irish Republican Brotherhood, better known as Fenianism, first took root in Dublin in 1858 although it actually originated with Irish emigrants to North America who continued to provide it with financial aid throughout its existence. Although some of its members had previously been active in Young Ireland, as a movement it initially rejected any firm commitment to land reform. It was futile, insisted leaders like Charles Kickham, to hope for this 'as long as Ireland continued to be ruled by a foreign government'. Indeed, during the 1860s, a strong anti-rural sentiment permeated much of its propaganda which portrayed tenant farmers as selfish individuals unconcerned about the plight of the rest of the population. Not surprisingly, Fenianism developed as a town-based movement, at least for the first twenty years of its existence, recruiting most successfully among young artisans and members of the lower middle classes. Samuel Clark's analysis of suspected Fenians operating between 1866 and 1871 identified only 22 per cent from rural backgrounds, nearly half of them general labourers.[6] Only 10 per cent of those arrested after the unsuccessful uprising of 1867 were from the countryside and only 4 per cent of those ultimately brought to trial were farmers or farmers' sons.

A land question, therefore, while it contributed significantly to

Ireland's unruliness and disorder before the famine, did not provide the motive force behind political or nationalist mobilization, and by the time Gladstone declared his intention in 1868 to pacify Ireland, agrarian outrages had been reduced dramatically and farming was generally prosperous. Any hopes that a reform of land tenure would reduce nationalist sentiment and support must be considered misplaced. Indeed, within a decade of Gladstone's Land Act of 1870 Ireland was engulfed in a protracted, bitter land war led, in the main, by committed nationalists. How had this come about and how did its organization, aims and support differ from the campaigns of the earlier agrarian societies who had disappeared with the famine?

THE LAND WAR, 1879–82

By the 1850s, changes in land laws were increasingly championed by what one Kilkenny journalist described as 'a class of respectable and sturdy farmers who were possessed of competent means.' Their first initiative was the Irish Tenant League formed in 1849 as a reaction to a sharp, temporary drop in agricultural prices. The demands were very similar to the 3 'Fs' conceded thirty years later by Gladstone (see pp. 37–8): 'fair' rents, free sale (that is the right of an outgoing tenant to sell his right or interest in the holding on quitting a farm), and fixity of tenure (that is, legal recognition of a tenant's right to occupy a holding subject to the payment of rent and the observance of any reasonable conditions stipulated by the landlord). Its strategy was entirely constitutional, relying on an extension of the parliamentary franchise introduced in 1850 to secure the return of a party to state its case in London. In the election of 1852, forty-eight Irish MPs were returned on the League's ticket, but by March 1858 it had collapsed as a political force, split at Westminster over whether to accept compromise solutions and undermined at home by landlords' pressure and the agricultural prosperity of the 1850s. Local farmers' clubs, however, continued to expand throughout the 1860s and by the 1870s, political leaders, including some Fenians, were becoming aware of the importance of hitching the support of these associations' members to the nationalist waggon, even though they recognized the danger of getting side-tracked by farmers' rather narrow grievances. In 1870 the inter-denominational, broadly based Home Government Association was formed by a Tory lawyer, Isaac Butt, to promote parliamentary candidates pledged to limited devolution of power. It soon realized that, while the adoption of a programme of agrarian reform seemed to attract voters, especially in the 1874 parliamentary elections after the Secret Ballot Act of 1872 had removed any possibility of electoral influence exerted by landlords, there was a danger of alienating urban, propertied and Protestant landlord support. Nevertheless, on 1 June 1879 the new president of the retitled Home Rule Confederation, Charles Stewart Parnell, had joined forces with some of the more radical Fenians in a 'New Departure' which pledged support to farmers in their fight for land reform.

The reason for this expedient was the unprecedented scale of farmers' mobilization, throughout Ireland, calling for immediate redress of grievances and land reform. This activity was precipitated by the downturn in farming fortunes after 1877 (see pp. 9–10) and it originated in the western counties which had previously taken little part in either political or economic associations. The smallholders there were soon joined by more substantial tenant farmers from the rest of Ireland. Support was most evident in the predominantly pastoral areas of south Leinster and Munster, especially in the county of Kerry where livestock farming co-existed with a substantial residual smallholding economy, but the vexed question of tenant right, which Gladstone's legislation of 1870 had done little to solve (see pp. 36–7), also persuaded many Ulster farmers to join the movement during 1879 and 1880.

Although local leaders were drawn from the farming community or from among town-based tradesmen who relied on agriculture for their own prosperity, the potential of this upsurge of popular discontent was quickly recognized by nationalist leaders who saw it, in Joseph Lee's words, as 'the engine which would draw Home Rule in its train'.[2] Some of the old guard of Fenian leaders like Charles Kickham condemned the protest as mere Whiteboyism and refused to associate themselves with it, but a significant number, including Michael Davitt, John O'Connor Power and John Devoy, now threw themselves into the campaign for land reform. Fearing that the constitutional movement for Home Rule would be outflanked, Parnell joined them in a marriage of convenience in June 1879. A haughty Protestant landlord from Wicklow and MP for Meath from 1874, Parnell viewed this as an opportunity to obtain popular support to strengthen his claim, which at that time was far from secure, to be undisputed leader of the Irish parliamentary party, and to moderate some of the Fenian demands. He also seems to have hoped, rather forlornly as it turned out, that land reform which undermined the economic position of the landowners would persuade them to abandon their support for the British government and join the nationalist camp.

In October 1879 the Irish National Land League was established to co-ordinate activity, with Parnell as its president, and in the spring of the following year he, Davitt and John Dillon visited the United States on a fund-raising tour. The return of a Liberal administration in the general election of April 1880 and the triumph of Parnellite candidates in Ireland seemed to promise a speedy solution to the problem. In January 1881 two Royal Commissions submitted reports which dealt at length with the situation in Ireland. The Royal Commission on Agriculture under the chairmanship of the Duke of Richmond had been set up in the summer of 1879 by Disraeli's government to examine the agricultural depression throughout the United Kingdom and had visited Ireland in the summer of 1880. The Liberals' Bessborough Commission had only begun its work in September 1880 but its brief was restricted to Irish matters and it was able to complete its work more quickly. Both recommended reforms, but Gladstone felt compelled to restore public order before introducing them and the Protection of Person and Property Act was passed in March 1881. Nationalist leaders continued to urge their supporters to maintain their protests despite the subsequent passage of the Land Act in August 1881 (see pp. 37–9). As a result many of them, including Parnell, were arrested in October and the League itself suppressed. As outrages escalated during the winter of 1881–2, both the British government and Parnell sought a compromise. This was finally reached in the Kilmainham Treaty of 1882, called after the jail in which the leaders had been held. In return for his release and the promise of a further act extending the provisions of the 1881 Land Act to include tenants in arrears with their rent, Parnell agreed to cease active campaigning on the issue. Although continued disturbances are recorded for the rest of the century, by the autumn of 1882 the Land War was effectively over.

No other aspect of the land problem has received such scholarly scrutiny as the events of 1879–82, yet the answers to several important questions are still far from clear. Three in particular deserve special attention here. Why was this particular depression accompanied by such concerted national agitation when earlier depressions and the terrible years of famine were not? What were the aims, tactics and social composition of the movement and how did they differ from those of earlier rural organizations? What were the long-term implications for Irish society and the nationalist movement?

Historians are closer to consensus on the first aspect than the other two. The traditional view, which can be traced back to the League's own propaganda, that this was the reaction of a poverty-stricken peasantry to mounting landlord exploitation, excessive rents and widespread evictions, has been largely discredited (see pp. 17–22). As we have seen, rents had lagged behind profit levels since the famine and, until the Land War itself, evictions were few. It was rather a revolution of rising expectations, a desire to hold on to the considerable gains of the previous thirty years. When landlords, faced with irreducible interest payments on their debts, proved unwilling or unable to reduce rents sufficiently, redress was sought.

In pre-famine Ireland the conflicting interest of smallholders and the expanding grazier class had been at the centre of rural protest; in the Land War they both appeared to be on the same side, ranged against landlords. For Samuel Clark, this 'challenging collectivity' was the most significant feature of the agitation; 'The most outstanding difference was the extent to which the poor landholders in the west became mobilized. The unprecedented feature of the Land War was the formation of a national-associational active collectivity composed of tenant farmers.'[6] Others, notably Paul Bew, while agreeing that it was indeed a broadly based tenant farmers' movement embracing both smallholders and larger graziers with virtually no involvement from the labouring class, have emphasized 'the existence of a considerable degree of peasant disunity within the overall anti-landlord unity of the Land League framework'.[5] Bew's contention is that the smallholders' demands for land redistribution were pushed aside from mid-1880 by substantial farmers seeking instead to consolidate their position by obtaining the three 'Fs' – fair rents, fixity of tenure and free sale – none of them particularly relevant at the time to tenants whose holdings were incapable of supporting them. Resolutions passed at Land League conferences suggest that Bew's emphasis on changing priorities has some substance.

The League's tactics also changed and varied between regions. Some of the many strategies adopted resembled those of pre-famine Whiteboyism – assault, intimidation, collective resistance to and reprisals for evictions. The incidence of such outrages seems to have been higher in the less developed west of Ireland and to have risen during times when nationally co-ordinated activity was flagging. The dominant strategy of the League from the summer of 1880, however, was designed to be non-violent. Boycotting, which takes its name from one of its earliest victims, Captain Boycott, involved social ostracism and passive resistance. To maintain pressure on landlords' finances without incurring the risk of eviction, larger farmers withheld payments of rent until all legal recourses had been exhausted and the bailiffs arrived, a policy referred to as 'rent at the point of a bayonet'. After Gladstone had substantially met the demands of this group with his Land Act of August 1881, the 'No Rent' manifesto issued by Parnell and other imprisoned leaders in October 1881 fell on deaf ears. The presence of what Emmet Larkin has called 'the nation forming class' of medium to large farmers among the ranks of the Land Leaguers seems to have been a major influence on tactics and, probably, the most significant factor in the League's success.[18]

The crucial importance of the Land League for the nationalist movement has been widely asserted but neither adequately explained nor convincingly supported. The political consciousness of the rank and file in any popular movement is always difficult to assess so the undisputed support for nationalist leaders, who championed the farmers' cause after 1879, does not necessarily imply that the two causes were equally popular despite the nationalists' frequent protestations that the two issues were inextricably linked. It is clear that the popular picture of poverty and exploitation breeding virulent anti-English feelings is erroneous, although this does not exclude the possibility that past injustices, real or imagined, played a significant role in mobilizing opinion or, indeed, in influencing British policy. Nationalism might more profitably be interpreted as a consequence of increasing literacy and prosperity which kindled an Irish self-confidence which British concessions on agrarian, educational and religious matters heightened rather than satisfied. The Land War in such an analysis could be viewed, not as a cause, but as a symptom, albeit a major one, of more important forces at work in Irish society.

On the one hand, it does not seem feasible to explain the electoral success of 1885, when Parnell's party won eighty-five seats, without reference to the Land War. This had confirmed and exalted Parnell, whatever his faults, as the recognized leader of Irish constitutional nationalism. The Irish National League which superseded the Land League in October 1882 built upon its predecessor's branch structure and formed the basis of a coherent, organized political party such as Ireland had not seen before. The success of the land campaign also undoubtedly boosted Irish self-confidence and esteem, shattering any vestigial deference or subservience. Its emphasis on traditional rights of settlement fostered an historical sense of national identity, an emotion further nurtured by the qualified blessing bestowed upon the movement by the Catholic Church.

Yet the relationship between the land question and nationalism still remains complex and problematical. It is significant that between 1879 and 1882 resolutions at the Land League's conferences calling for some form of self-government were heavily outnumbered by those concerned with land reform. The British government's failure to check the development of nationalist feeling with a series of wide-ranging land acts strengthens the impression that this relied on other factors than the land for its appeal. It is to the search for a legislative solution that we now turn.

The British government and the land question

Fundamental to British policy towards Ireland throughout the nineteenth century was a belief that economic prosperity was a panacea for Irish social and political unrest. Land reform seemed to promise to remove both perceived barriers to improvement and modernization and to resolve the underlying problem of Irish insubordination. As Gladstone remarked in 1870, it was his 'high and ardent' hope that Ireland would be united to England and Scotland 'by the only enduring ties of free will and free affection, peace, order and a settled and cheerful industry'. Any assessment of land policy, therefore, must take into account the degree to which various measures did in fact encourage prosperity, lessen social disorder and provide the antidote to burgeoning nationalism. Unfortunately both the solutions proposed and the legislation introduced were incapable of achieving all three objectives concurrently. Some measures were to prove irrelevant, others positively counter-productive.

PROPOSED SOLUTIONS

1 Larger more efficient farms

Political economists, especially in the first half of the century, regularly advocated amalgamation and consolidation of holdings on the English model. Hutches Trower, in a letter to David Ricardo in 1822, summarized this view most effectively:

It appears to me, that no permanent or substantial good can be done till all small farms and small tenancies are got rid of. They are the curse of Ireland. They are calculated to destroy that wholesome dependence of the lower upon the upper classes which is one of the master links of society; and to encourage habits of idleness, which are the bane of all moral feeling. I am aware, there would be difficulty in carrying this measure into execution, but the object is most important. The two deficiencies in Ireland are *want of capital* and *want of industry*. By destroying small tenancies you would obtain both.

As J. L. Hammond commented sardonically over 100 years later, 'The right policy then was, not to try and make the peasant efficient but to abolish him. The magic word was clearance.'[17]

The execution of this process was considered to be the landlords' responsibility with the state's role limited to providing a suitable legal framework. The Ejection Act of 1816 simplified the process of using the county courts for eviction; the introduction of the Subletting Act ten years later outlawed this practice. By relieving the poor man of the need to rely on potato plots for survival, the system of poor relief introduced in 1838 was, in the words of Sir George Cornewall Lewis, Chancellor of the Exchequer, intended to 'loosen his hold upon the land and thus relieve the landlord from the incubus which now presses upon him'. Despite landlords' sympathy with the government's aims and some progress in this quarter, the real breakthrough came when the famine brutally destroyed the ability of the smallholders to resist. The disaster also overwhelmed and impoverished many landlords, reducing their capacity to capitalize on the clearance. The Encumbered Estates Act of 1849 was intended to remedy this by allowing them to raise capital more easily and by introducing new funds and faces into the top ranks of rural society. Only with the re-emergence of problems on the over-crowded western seaboard in the 1880s was the government to intervene directly in order to create larger, more viable holdings. As well as attempting to attract investment to the area, the Congested District Boards, established under a Conservative administration in 1891, also purchased land for redistribution to form larger tenanted holdings.

As a remedy for economic backwardness, the patchy and incomplete implementation of this policy probably had its merits. Over the century it enabled farm output and productivity to rise and facilitated the shift to a market-orientated, profitable, pastoral economy. Socially, its effects are ambiguous. On the one hand, it strengthened the respectable, law-abiding class of medium-sized tenant farmers. On the other, its application in pre-famine Ireland inflamed rather than soothed social discontent since alternative industrial employment, which the economists recognized must accompany the clearances, did not materialize, and emigration, significant though it was, fell below the level necessary to cream off all the unwanted hordes of smallholders and cottiers. Although rural violence declined by the 1850s, the larger farmers, who had benefited from amalgamation of holdings, increasingly demanded better conditions and it was their grievances which came to dominate the land question. The Conservatives' belated attempts after 1891 to solve the problems of the west foundered on the same rocks which had wrecked earlier attempts to revitalize the economy – insufficient investment and employment for those denied access to land. The west's poverty was relieved to some extent but the hoped for economic rejuvenation did not materialize and emigration increased. Ireland's agricultural economy and the substantial tenant farmers may have prospered, therefore, but the majority of the Irish people enjoyed only the dubious benefit of being 'liberated' from the land. Nationalist feelings among both the larger farmers and the dispossessed, especially those who were forced to flee overseas, became more, rather than less pronounced as the century progressed.

2   State or co-operative ownership of land

Neither of these options attracted widespread support in Ireland, nor was either ever seriously considered by the British government. In the 1830s, Owenite Socialism, with its plans for co-operative ownership, made little headway in Ireland despite its temporary popularity in other parts of Britain. Various schemes for limited state purchase of land for resettlement were proposed from the 1840s by, among others, J. S. Mill, but all were still-born. In the early 1880s Michael Davitt's calls for state ownership fell on deaf ears. Only from the 1890s, as part of its solution to the problem of congested districts, did the government get involved in the land market in a small way. Problems of apathy and finance dogged all these plans. Farmers did not relish the prospect of dealing with an impersonal, distant landlord. Very few politicians ever considered such a state role to be practical or desirable since it was contrary to the dominant belief in the importance of private property. It is also difficult to imagine how the massive funds required for purchase, compensation and necessary agricultural investment could have been raised without incurring political unpopularity.

3   Changes in land tenure

4   Owner-occupancy

Both these options were strenuously pursued by British governments after 1870 and therefore, require rather more detailed assessments.

Gladstone was the first prominent Liberal politician to take an active interest in the position of the Irish tenant farmer. Ever since 1836, however, when Sharman Crawford had introduced a bill requiring landowners to compensate tenants for improvements, there had been numerous attempts to legislate on the land question, especially during the famine years. Most were frustrated by landowners' opposition in the House of Lords or by politicians' acknowledged ignorance of what was required. Only Cardwell's and Deasy's proposals reached the statute book, both in 1860. The former act stipulated that only written contracts, not agreements based on generally accepted custom, would be recognized in courts of law; the latter introduced compensation for improvements which outgoing tenants had carried out on their holdings so long as the investment had been approved in advance by the landlords.

Throughout the first thirty-six years of his political life Gladstone showed no constructive interest in solving the Irish question. He did not participate in debates over land reform, opposed Peel's increased grant to the Catholic Maynooth seminary in 1844 and, as Chancellor of the Exchequer, even extended income tax to Ireland in 1853, eleven years after Peel had introduced it in England. All his life he was to hold the Irish in contempt and he only ever visited their country once, in 1877, apparently coming home none the wiser or more tolerant for his expedition. Viewed in this light, his espousal of the mission to pacify Ireland at the time of the 1868 election was both remarkable and unexpected. Various explanations for his conversion have been put forward: undisguised horror at the Fenian atrocities, especially those on the English mainland in 1867; a growing awareness, based on his understanding of European politics, of the potency of nationalist feelings; a sincere desire to bring peace to a troubled island. Gladstone himself maintained that he took up the cause for 'the God of truth and justice'; his opponents, probably with some justification, insisted that it was a political ploy designed to improve his party's electoral chances in Ireland and rally the divided Liberals everywhere behind a unifying cause. As H. C. G. Matthew's introduction to the published Gladstone diaries for this period has emphasized, the Liberal party which swept into power in 1868 was a fragile being, a coalition of diverse interest groups with narrow preconceptions.[19] This situation both required and allowed Gladstone to put forward a cause to bind them together under his leadership. Ireland was that cause, although by 1885 it was to have proved counter-productive.

Gladstone's intentions for Ireland itself seem rather clearer. Two points in particular need to be borne in mind. First, all his measures were designed, by bringing peace and prosperity to the country, to secure Irish acceptance of British political control. Second, he was dedicated to maintaining the landlord class there.In 1863 he had remarked that their 'social and moral influence' was 'absolutely essential to the welfare of the country'. This belief remained unshaken by subsequent events. In 1870 he expressed the hope that his legislation would bring about 'a state of things in which the landlords of Ireland may assume . . . the position which is happily held as a class by the landlords of this country'. Proposals to encourage owner-occupancy he always viewed with distaste and alarm. Although he felt obliged to include provision for it in his legislation of 1870 and 1881, he consistently opposed Conservative measures to promote it after 1886 and ignored it during his final ministry of 1892–5.

Whatever his intentions there can be no doubt about his commitment and energy. The Land Act of 1870 was the outcome of three months of hectic consultation and hard political bargaining. It contained the following major provisions:

1. Tenants' customary rights were to be recognized by law wherever it was agreed that they existed. Elsewhere, tenants leaving farms were to be compensated by landlords for improvements, now assumed to be theirs and not the landlords', and for eviction, unless this was for non-payment of rent.
2. The Act's provisions were not to apply to tenants who held their land on leases of 31 or more years, because they were assumed to have adequate protection by the terms of those leases.
3. Tenants wishing to buy their farms from amenable landowners were allowed to borrow up to two-thirds of the cost from the Commissioners of Public Works, paying the debt off at 5 per cent interest over 35 years.

However well-intentioned, it is now generally agreed this act was, at best, irrelevant, at worst counter-productive. The poor response to the measures concerned with owner-occupancy, included primarily to pacify John Bright, one of Gladstone's influential cabinet ministers, surprised no one; the terms were unfavourable and tenants lacked the necessary one-third deposit, and probably the desire, to buy. More significantly, it failed to satisfy the more substantial leasehold farmers who had spearheaded the campaigns for land reform. Indeed, many of them were excluded from the terms of the act. Disputes over the nature, the extent and even the existence of customary rights also poisoned landlord-tenant relationships since they were now fought in open court. In order to circumvent the legislation, landlords resorted to giving more long leases, which, while they gave tenants some security, often contained restrictive clauses and conditions. It was, as an English politician had feared, 'a boon to the lawyers of Ireland'. Furthermore, Gladstone refused to consider the farmers' main demand for rent control, consisting it an unwarrantable interference with landlords' property rights. Without this, there was nothing in principle to stop landlords raising rents to a competitive level, thus eroding the value of tenant right and undermining the measures providing compensation for improvements. The clauses dealing with security of tenure had no effect on evictions, which were already running at a low level. The continuing profitability of the early 1870s was based on favourable market trends and cannot be attributed to the act, although prosperity may have muted dissatisfaction with the legislation. Gladstone, however, on his visit to the country in 1877, considered that he had effected a permanent solution to the land question and declared himself 'quite contented' with 'the social condition of Ireland and the prospects of its future solid happiness'. His misplaced optimism was soon undermined, but the further concessions demanded by the Land League only served to strengthen his dislike of what he considered to be a selfish and ungrateful people.

The Liberals, on their return to power in 1880, were unprepared for the intensity of the agitation in Ireland; the crisis, commented Gladstone, 'rushed upon us like a flood'. Ignoring the majority report of the Richmond Commission which recommended a package of reforms including public assistance for emigration, resettlement, drainage and communications to improve Irish agriculture, Gladstone moulded his legislation on the conclusions of the Bessborough Commission which were favourable to the principles of the three 'Fs' demanded by the Land League. The complicated Land Act with its sixty-two clauses which finally became law in August 1881 should be viewed, in the words of Barbara Solow, 'as less an economic policy than a political stroke'.[11] It allowed tenants to appeal to new land courts which were empowered to fix legally binding 'fair' rents which would operate for fifteen years. It granted farmers security of tenure on their holdings, whatever their size, so long as the rent was paid, and it confirmed the right of tenants to sell their interest in a holding at the best market price without interference from their landlords. The Arrears of Rent Act the following year extended these provisions to cover the estimated 130,000 tenants then in arrears, allowing them to apply for retrospective reductions in their rents. With these measures, Liberal initiatives on the land question ceased.

The political significance of this legislation of 1881–2 is still widely debated. The legislative interference with previously inviolable property rights was unprecedented. Some historians have suggested that this, and not Gladstone's subsequent declaration in favour of Home Rule in 1885, was primarily responsible for the decline of the British Liberal Party, with both urban and rural property owners drifting into the safety of the Conservative camp. In Ireland it certainly undermined immediate support for the Land League but nationalist candidates continued to do well in elections, mainly at the expense of the Liberals who were all but wiped out in 1885, even in Ulster, as opinion polarized between Home Rulers and Unionists.

The impact on Irish agriculture appears to have been negligible. It did nothing to solve the problems of the smallholders in the west whose unsated land hunger was reflected in a continuing, intermittent land war demanding land redistribution. Since most tenant farmers already enjoyed the traditional rights of free sale and fixity of tenure, the legalization of such customs made little difference. Rents, the main bone of contention despite their low level, were further reduced by an average of 20 per cent, but this was a consequence of decisions of the land courts rather than the intention of the legislators. No incentives were given to improve agricultural efficiency. Instead the inefficient tenant was given legal protection and all farmers were encouraged to turn to the courts for rent reductions to improve or maintain their incomes rather than to improve productivity and lower costs. In the long run the revival of farming fortunes from the mid-1880s and the subsequent development of Irish agriculture owed more to market forces than to any legal tinkering with rents or tenure. Landlordism, however, already on the wane and far less pernicious and oppressive than it was frequently portrayed, was dealt a blow by the Land Act of 1881 from which it never recovered. With their control of estates diminished and their power to fix rents· abolished, landowners had every incentive to sell out. That no massive transfer of land occurred immediately was due entirely to the fact that tenant farmers were now in such a favourable position that they had no incentive to buy. It was left to later Conservative administrations to bridge the gap between the prices at which landlords were prepared to sell and the sums which tenants were prepared to offer. It was their legislative measures, not those of the Liberals, which transformed the face of rural Ireland, measures which the ageing Gladstone was to condemn as 'dangerous and mischievous'.

BALFOUR AND THE CONSERVATIVES

After 1885 Gladstonian Liberals committed themselves to the idea of introducing a restricted form of devolved government, Home Rule, into Ireland. This, they hoped, would be sufficient to silence more radical demands for complete independence and would allow the British government to retain ultimate responsibility for foreign affairs and commerce. The Conservatives and Liberal Unionists refused to contemplate even such a limited separation and continued to search for other concessions to undermine nationalist support. Peasant proprietorship, or owner-occupancy, seemed to promise to achieve this.

Measures to encourage tenants to purchase their holdings had been proposed as early as the 1840s by John Bright and J. S. Mill in London, and by Young Irelanders like James Fintan Lalor in Dublin. Minor provisions in the acts of 1870 and 1881 making small loans available to tenants had been largely ineffective, however, and Gladstone declared himself unwilling to make further sums available in 1882, declaring that the Irish tenant farmer could not 'be safely accepted as a debtor on a large scale to the Imperial treasury'. Farmers consequently proved unwilling to contemplate purchase as their tenant rights on the land were confirmed; they had no irresistible, romantic view of the unmixed blessings of proprietorship. Land Leaguers and nationalists also disagreed among themselves on the appropriateness of such a venture. James Daly, an active Land Leaguer and the editor of the influential *Connaught Times*, told the Bessborough Commission in 1880: 'If you give the facilities to create peasant proprietorship you would make the peasant more conservative than the Conservatives.'

To the Conservatives this seemed an eminently admirable outcome. Demoralized, impoverished landlords increasingly supported the idea of a rescue operation which involved utilizing taxpayers' money to subsidize purchases by making loans available to tenants on favourable terms. The old landowning class could then retire gracefully on the proceeds while the new farming landowners in this property-owning

39

democracy would, it was hoped, become defenders of the *status quo*, upholders of law and order and supporters of British rule.

As early as March 1882 a Conservative MP, W. H. Smith, announced his intention of introducing a bill 'to facilitate the transfer of ownership of land to occupiers on terms which would be just and reasonable to the existing landlords'. Under the Ashbourne Act of 1885 the British government allocated £5 million to provide loans to tenants who wished to purchase their holdings from landlords who had expressed a willingness to sell; no compulsion was involved. Terms were far more generous for the tenant than those included in earlier acts. Only two-thirds of the purchase price could be advanced under the 1870 act, three-quarters under that of 1881 but after 1885 the entire transaction could be funded by a treasury loan. The rate of interest charged was also reduced from 5 per cent charged under previous legislation to just 4 per cent, and the time allowed for repayment lengthened from 35 to 49 years, thus considerably reducing a borrower's annual outgoings. The initiative was continued by Arthur Balfour, Chief Secretary for Ireland between March 1887 and November 1891 and nephew of the then prime minister, Lord Salisbury, whom he succeeded in 1902. First, an amending act providing a further £5 million under the terms of the 1885 act was passed in December 1888 and then the Land Purchase Act of August 1891 increased the funding to £33 million but introduced less attractive conditions. Although the rate of interest and length of repayment remained unaltered, tenants were now provided with government stock, rather than cash, with which to pay the landlords. After various modifications to the scheme in 1896, a major breakthrough occurred in 1903, during Balfour's own administration. The Irish Land Purchase Act, commonly referred to as the Wyndham Act after the then Irish Secretary, adopted the recommendations of a joint landlord-tenant conference of the previous year which had met in Dublin under the chairmanship of the Earl of Dunraven. The rate of interest was reduced to 3.25 per cent and the term of repayment increased to sixty-eight and a half years. Tenants were assured that repayments would be below existing rent levels. Cash advances replaced the unpopular loan stock. Landlords were encouraged to sell entire estates rather than piecemeal holdings and were given a 12 per cent bonus on the selling price from British government funds. A Liberal sponsored amendment of 1909, Birrell's Land Act, provided additional finance.

Together these acts transformed the pattern of landownership in Ireland, although it was not until after 1903 that sales increased from a trickle to a flood. Only 877 tenants took advantage of the clauses in the 1870 act, a further 731 those of the 1881 measures. Around 25,000 applied for money in the six years after the Ashbourne Act and a further 35,000 after 1891 and 1896. The Wyndham Act resulted in nearly 300,000 sales, 100,000 of them between 1906 and 1908, and by the time of the First World War an estimated two-thirds to three-quarters of farmers owned their own holdings. Legislation introduced by the new Irish Free State in 1923 compelled remaining landlords to sell. In the rest of the United Kingdom where government funding was not made available, the expansion of owner-occupancy proceeded at a much slower pace than in Ireland and was far from complete by the 1920s. Conservative legislation, therefore, helped to effect a speedy, but rather painless end to landlordism in Ireland.

'As the last act in the history of the Irish Land Question was being played out,' concludes Barbara Solow, 'the tragic irrelevance of the drama was plain to see.'[11] Although R. D. Crotty has suggested that the favourable terms granted to owner-occupiers sheltered the less efficient from the chill winds of competition and retarded economic progress, others, notably Joseph Lee, have pointed out that this was already the case, since tenants enjoyed low rents and security of tenure. Land purchase, like changes in land tenure, did nothing to improve the conditions of the smallholding economy in the west of the country. The British optimism that Home Rule could be killed by kindness proved to be misplaced. Perhaps the legislation came too late, although this hypothesis implies that earlier measures would have been successful, a theory it is impossible to test but possible to doubt. The history of disagreements over land does not suggest that these ever provided the foundation for the Irish nationalist movement. It would be wrong, therefore, to expect that economic palliatives could ever have checked the development of an increasingly self-confident, cultural, emotional nationalism.

Conclusion

This pamphlet set out to survey three aspects of Irish history in the nineteenth century: the accuracy of the traditional view of rural society; the possible relationship between the land system and Irish agricultural backwardness, social unrest and nationalism; and the appropriateness and impact of British legislation dealing with the land question. It has deliberately avoided concentrating directly on the famine of 1845–9, undoubtedly the most dramatic landmark and, in many interpretations, the most influential and decisive event of the century. Instead, it has endeavoured to place this tragedy, and other equally well recognized landmarks, in a long-term overview of economic and political development.

Clearly, conditions in Ireland in the early twentieth century were vastly different from those which had prevailed 100 years earlier. Population, which had risen to a peak of nearly 8.2 million in 1841, had shrunk dramatically to just under 4.5 million in 1901 and was still falling. Domestic industry had all but disappeared and Ireland, with the exception of a few large towns, had become almost entirely dependent on farming. Medium-sized farms, a steadily increasing percentage of them owned rather than rented by their occupiers, dominated the countryside; the virtually landless labourers and cottiers had all but disappeared from much of Ireland and with them the dire poverty and potato-dependent diet usually associated with the country. Pre-famine social structure and ways of life had survived only in the west. The majority of the Irish people were incomparably richer than their predecessors, even though their income per head was still one of the lowest in Europe.

This transformation was the culmination of a long period of change

42

rather than the consequence of one or two dramatic incidents. Although the famine greatly accelerated the pace of development, it did not lead to a marked change of direction. Population growth was already slackening off before 1845, arable land was being laid down to grass, farms were becoming bigger and emigration was common, especially in parts of Leinster and Munster. The British government's land reforms, while ultimately contributing to the rapid expansion of owner-occupancy, had little impact on agricultural efficiency or economic prosperity. The widely accepted, understandable practice of studying each country's domestic history in isolation has also, in Ireland's case, been unfortunate. It has resulted in an over-statement both of the uniqueness of her rural history and of the importance of the internal forces which determined its course. The saga of increasing farm sizes, pastoral specialization, declining rural population and the erosion of landed influence could equally well apply to Wales, Scotland or England. Since she increasingly possessed a far from self-contained, subsistence economy, Ireland's farmers were just as influenced by, and seemed to have shown the same responsiveness to, changing international market conditions. In many respects they were better placed than their English counterparts to exploit the growing demand for meat and dairy produce which accompanied British industrialization. The uniqueness of Ireland, and therefore its tragedy, was that no industrial development occurred within its boundaries to ease the pain of this transition and absorb its surplus rural population. In no way, however, can this failure be attributed to the inadequacies or otherwise of the land system. The traditional view that Irish development was retarded by the oppression and exploitation carried out by a small landowning class has been largely discredited by recent research.

The phenomena of rural violence and Irish nationalism also need to be viewed in their proper contexts. Agrarian unrest before the famine was certainly connected with the question of access to land, but it was a product, not of an unchanging, peasant society, but of a gradually evolving, modernizing economy. Agricultural imbalance and surplus population led to serious rural disturbances and high levels of crime in parts of England during the same period. Post-famine land agitation was very different and reflected the changing social structure of rural Ireland and the expectations of its inhabitants. Largely peaceful and constitutional, it was concerned with preserving recent economic gains and it was supported primarily by respectable, socially-aspiring farmers. The relationship between any of this concern over land and the nationalist movement was never more than fragile and temporary. Whiteboyism was essentially a collection of local rural protests by the poorer class while, as late as the 1860s, Fenians regarded tenant farmers' obsession with the land as an unwelcome diversion from the real political struggle for independence. Until the 1870s, nationalism was essentially a sophisticated, urban movement supported by the relatively wealthy and upwardly socially mobile. Only with the Land War after 1879 was there any concerted attempt to bring the two movements together.

The growth of nationalism, like the development of Irish agriculture, did not depend primarily on the land question. Ireland was not alone in Europe in seeking to break free from the political control of a foreign government, nor was it the first. Nationalist feelings increasingly pervaded most European states in the half century before 1914. Nor were Irish demands for Home Rule unique within the British Empire. Australia, New Zealand and Canada had all enjoyed internal self-government from the mid-Victorian period and, along with the Union of South Africa, were to obtain dominion status around the turn of the twentieth century. What turned Irish Home Rule into such a protracted political squabble was not the peculiar strength of the nationalists, or even their presence at Westminster, but the stubbornness with which a substantial section of the British political élite and the Protestant minority in Ulster resisted.

The importance of the famine in the development of popular nationalism does not lie in any immediate impact it had in Ireland. There is no evidence to prove that those who suffered at the time blamed the English for their plight; oral tradition suggests, rather, a fatalistic acceptance of a natural disaster. Both O'Connell's Repeal Association and the militant Young Ireland movement were crushed rather than inflated by the crisis and rural pressure groups of the 1850s, like those of the pre-famine decades, were concerned with narrow, sectional issues. The famine's place in nationalist history came later as it was re-interpreted by popular historians to provide justification for their movement. The first writer to do so would appear to have been John Mitchel in his book, *The Last Conquest of Ireland (Perhaps)* first published in 1860. It was he, claims Patrick O'Farrell, who ''invented'' the Great Irish Famine of 1845–9, that is, gave it initially the place it has come to occupy in commonly perceived historical and imaginative understanding'.[20] Later volumes, like Michael Davitt's *The Fall of Feudalism in Ireland* (1904) restated Mitchel's argument that, 'The Almighty indeed, sent the potato blight, but the English created the famine', and extended their critique to incorporate the long tradition of Irish rural protest into a nationalist framework. It is a tribute to the persuasive artistry of such works that their interpretation of Irish history still has so many supporters on both sides of the Irish Sea.

Despite this revised view of the importance of the land question for both Irish agricultural development and most nineteenth-century nationalist movements, it does not follow that it should be dismissed as an historical irrelevancy. Belief in its centrality to the Irish issue had a profound effect on British economists' and politicians' approach to Ireland. As has just been suggested, it has also been instrumental in forging and sustaining a powerful, nationalist interpretation of Irish development. This success alone is sufficient justification for examining the validity of the account. For the historian, the discrepancy which such an examination reveals between the popular image and the reality of nineteenth-century Ireland, suggests that new approaches are needed if we are fully to appreciate the nature and development of Irish national consciousness.

Select Bibliography

GENERAL TEXTS (all available in paperback)

1. G. Ó Tuathaigh, *Ireland Before the Famine, 1798–1848* (Dublin, 1972).
2. J. Lee, *The Modernisation of Irish Society, 1848–1918* (Dublin, 1973).
3. F. S. L. Lyons, *Ireland Since the Famine* (London, 1973).

RECENT WORKS ON THE LAND QUESTION

4. M. R. Beames, *Peasants and Power: The Whiteboy Movement and its control in Pre-Famine Ireland* (Hassocks, 1983).
5. P. Bew, *Land and the National Question in Ireland, 1858–82* (Dublin, 1979).
6. S. Clark, *Social Origins of the Irish Land War* (Princeton, 1979).
7. R. D. Crotty, *Irish Agricultural Production* (Cork, 1966).
8. J. M. Goldstrom, 'Irish agriculture and the Great Famine', in J. M. Goldstrom and L. A. Clarkson (eds.), *Irish Population, Economy and Society* (Oxford, 1981).
9. J. Lee, 'Irish Agriculture', *Agricultural History Review*, xvii, 1969.
10. J. Mokyr, *Why Ireland Starved* (London, 1983).
11. B. Solow, *The Land Question and the Irish Economy, 1870–1903* (Harvard, 1971).
12. W. E. Vaughan, 'Landlord and tenant relations in Ireland between the famine and the Land War, 1850–1878', in L. M. Cullen and T. C. Smout (eds.) *Comparative Aspects of Scottish and Irish Economic and Social History, 1600–1900* (Edinburgh, 1977).

OTHER WORKS CITED IN THE TEXT

13. P. M. A. Bourke, 'The agricultural statistics of the 1841 census', *Economic History Review*, xviii, 1965.

14. S. J. Connolly, *Priests and People in pre-Famine Ireland, 1780–1845* (Dublin, 1982).
15. L. M. Cullen, *An Economic History of Ireland since 1660* (London, 1972).
16. J. S. Donnelly, *The Land and People of Nineteenth-Century Cork* (London, 1975).
17. J. L. Hammond, *Gladstone and the Irish Nation* (London, 1938).
18. E. Larkin, 'Church, state and nation in modern Ireland', *American Historical Review*, lxxx, 1975.
19. H. C. G. Matthew (ed.), *The Gladstone Diaries*, vol. vii (Oxford, 1982).
20. P. O'Farrell, 'Whose reality? The Irish famine in history and literature', *Historical Studies of Australia and New Zealand*, xx, 1982.